Offender-Desistance Policing
and the Sword of Damocles

Offender-Desistance Policing and the Sword of Damocles

Lawrence W. Sherman
and
Peter W. Neyroud

Commentary by
Ken Pease

Civitas: Institute for the Study of Civil Society
London

First Published May 2012

© Civitas 2012
55 Tufton Street
London SW1P 3QL

email: books@civitas.org.uk

ISBN 978-1-906837-38-9

Independence: Civitas: Institute for the Study of Civil Society is a registered educational charity (No. 1085494) and a company limited by guarantee (No. 04023541). Civitas is financed from a variety of private sources to avoid over-reliance on any single or small group of donors.

All publications are independently refereed. All the Institute's publications seek to further its objective of promoting the advancement of learning. The views expressed are those of the authors, not of the Institute.

Typeset by
Civitas

Printed in Great Britain by
Berforts Group Ltd
Stevenage SG1 2BH

Contents

Authors

Lawrence W. Sherman was elected Wolfson Professor of Criminology of the University of Cambridge in 2006. He has been president of the American Society of Criminology, the International Society of Criminology, the American Academy of Political and Social Science, and the Academy of Experimental Criminology. His research interests are in the fields of crime prevention, evidence-based policy, restorative justice, police practices and experimental criminology. He has conducted field experiments, for example, on finding more effective ways to reduce homicide, gun violence, domestic violence, robbery, burglary, and other crime problems, in collaboration with such agencies as the Metropolitan, Northumbria and Thames Valley Police, London's Crown Courts, HM Prisons, the Crown Prosecution Service, the Youth Justice Board of England and Wales, and the National Probation Service.

Peter W. Neyroud was the Chief Constable of Thames Valley from 2002-2006, a Vice-President of the ACPO and the Chief Executive of the National Policing Improvement Agency from 2006-10. He has been a member of the Sentencing Guidelines Council, Parole Board, National Policing Board and National Criminal Justice. In 2010 he was asked by the Home Secretary to carry out a 'fundamental review of Police Leadership and Training'. His Review proposed radical change and the establishment of a new professional body for policing, which has since been accepted by the Government. Since leaving the Police Service at the end of 2010 he has been carrying out a major research programme at Cambridge University into Crime Harm and is providing training, leadership development and consultancy nationally and internationally. He was awarded the QPM in 2004 and a CBE in 2011. He is a Visiting Professor at Chester University.

Ken Pease, of the Manchester Business School, is an internationally acclaimed criminologist. He has acted as a consultant to a number of organisations including the United Nations, the Council of Europe and the Customs Co-operation Council. He is also a former Parole Board member. He is the author of the Civitas reports: *Prison, Community Sentencing and Crime* (2010) and *Crime in England and Wales: More Violence and More Chronic Victims* (2007).

Summary

This paper outlines the concept of Offender-Desistance Policing (ODP), with specific reference to the criminological theory and evidence that underpins it. It then describes the programme of field experiments that are planned to develop the concept. In the third section, the paper summarises some of the specific tactics that police and partner agencies can test to increase offenders' likelihood of desisting from crime.

1

Policing and Criminal Justice Context in 2011[*]

Criminal justice agencies ranging from police to prisons are under increasing scrutiny both to reduce expenditure and enhance the cost-effectiveness of their operations. The UK government has set out a programme for reducing public expenditure, which presents the criminal justice agencies with the most challenging fiscal environment in living memory. Government policy papers on policing and reducing offending have laid a new stress on prevention, rehabilitation of offenders and on cost-effective approaches. Additionally there have been key changes to the responsibility of the police for making

---

[*] This essay is a revised version of Sherman, Lawrence W., 'Offender Desistance Policing (ODP): less prison and more evidence in rehabilitating offenders', in Bliesener, T., Beelmann, A. and Stemmler, M. (eds), *Antisocial Behavior and Crime: contributions of developmental and evaluation research to prevention and intervention*, Cambridge, MA: Hogrefe Publishing, 2011, pp. 199-218.

prosecution decisions. Proposals to expand this include decision-making for conditional cautioning, changes aimed at reducing bureaucracy and providing swift judicial responses to offending. Taken together, the government's fiscal policy and the reinforced focus on prevention provide an opportunity to consider how police and other agencies could more effectively intervene to prevent offending, deter offenders and encourage them to desist from further offending.

The Inspectorates (HMIC and Criminal Justice Inspectorate) have published a review of current practice of the use of alternatives to prosecution.[1] The findings, which were based on a small sample (not randomly selected), indicate that alternatives to prosecution (ranging from cautioning to Penalty Notices for Disorder): are at least as effective as prosecution when reoffending rates (after 12 months) are compared; compare very favourably on victim satisfaction (restorative justice approaches appear substantially better); and are significantly cheaper (even if the only costs compared are those for police time in the custody suite). The Inspection identified areas for improvement in the consistency of practice and recording of the results on the Police National Computer.

One point that the Inspection report did not address is the comparative paucity of high-quality research in the UK on the effectiveness of cautioning and alternatives to prosecution. With the exception of restorative justice, which has been the subject of a series of randomized experiments,[2] cautioning, conditional cautioning and other alternatives have not been the focus of the sort of systematic research attention that should have been provided to disposals that account for nearly half of the cases dealt with by the police. The Inspection report recommends the development of more consistent guidelines, but, as this paper will argue, it is overdue that these are underpinned by more robust evidence and experimentation.

2

Offender-Desistance Policing (ODP)

The key question is whether the police can cause more offenders to desist from crime through better use of pre-court disposals and, moreover, whether they can do so in a more effective way than prisons or even probation? Can police even *rehabilitate* offenders by *diversion* better than the processes of prosecution, sentencing and punishment? Can police safely divert a majority of apprehended offenders from prosecution by using a statistical forecasting tool to identify non-dangerous defendants? Is this a more cost-effective approach than prosecution? These are the key questions that can be answered by a programme of field experiments.

The indirect evidence suggesting that ODP might work comes from a variety of sources. The most basic source is *life-course criminology.* This work complements other literature on crime-harm forecasting for individual offenders, a recent systematic review of the effects of prosecution on recidivism, more wide-ranging reviews of the effects of prison on recidivism, a recent experiment testing greater certainty and celerity on probation; and the growing literature on offender-focused policing, including restorative policing.

Life-Course Criminology

The growing body of theory and evidence on crime across the life-course has been increasingly powerful in shaping many fields of criminology. While it has been remarkably absent from policing, there is good reason for its application. Its most visible findings are associated with the longest time-span over the lives of any sample of offenders, the group of 500 Massachusetts delinquents who have now been studied up to age 70.[1] The relevance of this study for policing is its evidence that desistance is a *process* more than a result, an off-and-on progression from more to less frequent and serious offending.[2] Life-course theory and concepts, such as turning points and the creation of new identities, help us to understand better how some people succeed in getting out of crime.

The implications of these findings for policing are huge. While courts and corrections may legally deal with offenders only on the basis of one case at a time, police are obliged to prevent crime at all times by all members of society. They are also obliged to use their scarce resources rationally. Despite political pressure on police to emphasise the *detection* of crime and the apprehension of offenders, it is in the public interest to prefer policing that prevents crime in the first place, just as Peel suggested. While 'incident-driven' policing in the standard police model[3] has little focus beyond a single crime, 'preventive policing' can build creatively upon a growing body of knowledge about entire criminal careers.

Using that knowledge, police may justifiably focus much of their effort on known offenders. The virtue of this focus is the high percentage of all crimes that are committed by this 'power few'.[4] This means that it may better serve the public interest to invest in the desistance of repeat offenders than in the investigation of specific cases, especially the majority of crimes that will never even be solved. The power of that hypothesis becomes even greater when the offenders in question may commit the most serious of crimes, such as murder and rape.

Crime-Harm Forecasting

While previous efforts to identify the most dangerous offenders have been disappointing, recent advances in event-forecasting methods have greatly improved the accuracy of such forecasts.[5] The capacity now exists, for example, to identify offenders on probation who generate 75 times more charges for murder or attempted murder than other offenders.[6] This capacity is based on the use of very large samples of criminal records, with tens of thousands of cases over multiple years. Because murder and other serious crimes are so rare, this kind of forecasting has not been possible with samples used for life-course criminology, typically with 500 to 10,000 cases in each sample. Crime-harm forecasting, in contrast, builds forecasting models with 30,000 cases or more,[7] using super-computers and non-linear methods to identify the most accurately predictive combinations of facts in the actuarial patterns of repeat offending.

The distinction between actuarial and clinical forecasting in this regard is critical. Police in many jurisdictions have tried to identify serious offenders using subjective, qualitatively 'clinical' methods. Yet every comparison between these methods and more quantitative methods has shown that clinical methods make more errors.[8] There are many reasons why police prefer clinical models, including the freedom to pursue hunches. But as the Chief Constable of a major police agency recently reported in her Master's thesis at Cambridge, the national clinical model for forecasting domestic homicide in Britain had a 100 per cent false negative rate over her years of experience in that agency. That is, not one domestic homicide or attempted homicide was committed by someone identified by a multi-agency effort as being at risk, despite thousands of potential offenders having been identified.

The harm forecasts from the most advanced statistical methods have already been applied in Pennsylvania and Maryland correctional agencies, and can readily be applied now in police agencies as well. In Philadelphia, for example, University of

Pennsylvania criminologist Geoffrey Barnes has integrated the Berk risk forecasting model with the Pennsylvania state criminal records system used in the Adult Probation and Parole Department. Using this software, probation intake staff are able to classify each offender as having a high, medium or low risk of committing a murder, attempted murder, rape or other sex crimes, robbery, or aggravated assault. Once the probationer's identification is entered into their computers, the classification is computed and reported to staff at their desks in 15 seconds. This capacity makes statistical harm forecasting not only more accurate than any other method, but also less expensive.

The best news about these advanced methods is this: the majority of offenders who are convicted and sentenced to probation or parole have very low risks of committing a very harmful crime. At least in Philadelphia, where the homicide rate was 27 per 100,000 at the time of the research, most offenders under court supervision pose no grave risks to public safety. Just as with the frequency of offending, the seriousness of offending is concentrated among a tiny fraction of all offenders.[9] Accordingly, the Philadelphia Probation Department has placed all of its clients into a risk-based system of triage using the Berk model.[10] A randomized experiment in lowering the investment of resources in the low-risk offenders showed no increase in offending among a sample of some 1,500 offenders.[11]

A randomized trial of cognitive behavioural therapy and intensive supervision for the high-risk offenders is under way, scheduled for completion in 2012 or 2013.

By implication, what can be done in probation can be done in policing. While police may not have court orders to enforce, they may have many other tools for negotiating with convicted and suspected offenders. Perhaps the most obvious opportunity is an arrest for a new crime, when it is possible for police to divert offenders from prosecution. When such opportunities arise, they can be informed by an evidence base that suggests less harm from diversion than from prosecution. Even without the benefits of precise harm forecasting, this evidence base suggests diversion. When combined with actuarial risk analysis, the value and safety of diversion may become even greater.

Effects of Prosecution on Recidivism

The practice of diversion from prosecution has been evaluated with repeated experiments in diverse communities for over four decades. These experiments have been mostly limited to juvenile offenders, but with more recent experiments including adults as well. The content of what suspects are diverted to has varied widely, but the comparison is always to (at least) full prosecution in court, with all the attrition that such cases entail. Attrition is found, of course, in both the diversion

9

programmes and criminal (or juvenile) prosecution. What the experiments all compare are the consequences of sending defendants down one pathway or another, rather than any particular treatment.

A systematic review of these experiments was recently published by the Campbell Collaboration's Crime and Justice Group.[12] Petrosino *et al.*'s review included 7,304 juveniles across 29 experiments reported over a 35-year period. They found that: 'almost all of the results are negative in direction, as measured by prevalence, incidence, severity, and self-report outcomes.' That is, prosecution in court appears to have no benefit in reducing repeat offending; instead, there is good evidence that it increases repeat offending. As a life-course turning point,[13] prosecution may be a very criminogenic experience for a young person.

Moreover, the benefit of diversion is derived simply from the prevention of prosecution. The more 'services' the juvenile was asked to receive, the less benefit there was from diversion. Across all studies reviewed, Petrosino *et al.*[14] found that the greatest benefit from diversion from prosecution occurred when suspects were simply told to stop offending, without any further requirements placed on them. This finding is startling and counter-intuitive to most people engaged with youth work. Yet it may fit the theory of defiance, especially if the young person distrusts the adults who are providing compulsory 'services' who they must obey in order to stay out of court. If replicated widely, this result would suggest that police may need to have the courage to do nothing, whenever the evidence shows that is the best thing that can be done.

Effects of Prison on Recidivism

The use of prosecution has a further potential harm as a gateway to imprisonment. Growing research evidence suggests that for many if not most people put in prison for the first time, the net effect of prison may be to cause more crime than if the sentence had not been custodial. In a series of very careful reviews of the effect of imprisonment on the imprisoned—which explicitly excludes the general deterrent effects of punishment—Daniel Nagin and his colleagues have concluded that there is virtually no good evidence that imprisonment 'works' over the life course of most offenders.[15] Reviewing what is admittedly non-experimental evidence, these scholars place the greatest emphasis on careful matching studies that examine offenders with similar criminal careers and instant offences. By comparing like-for-like offenders who go to prison with those who do not, they find no evidence that prison has a 'specific deterrent' effect. The findings reviewed include the 500 offenders who have been studied the longest, the Laub and Sampson sample of delinquents to age 70.[16]

What is even more important to police is the finding that prison creates no net incapacitation effect over an offender's career. Prison is generally said to 'work' as long as they remain in prison. But most prisoners come back into society. When they do, they can commit crimes at much higher rates than if they had never been sent to prison. The widespread assumption that offenders commit crimes at a constant rate is contradicted by the evidence. Even among offenders on trajectories of high offending, their frequencies may vary substantially over time.[17] An especially precise study in Amsterdam[18] found that the when offenders were sent to prison, their frequency of convictions rose so much (relative to offenders not sent to prison) that the incapacitation benefit was completely erased in only a few years; after that the net effect of imprisonment appeared to be that it caused more crime.

The vast majority of offenders in the advanced economies are not murderers or rapists, but drug-using property criminals. Many people, including victims, seek retribution for their crimes. But most would settle for anything that works, even if it is not prison. That is what makes the recent findings of a new experiment in probation so important.

Certainty and Celerity, Not Severity

The deterrence doctrine on which modern criminal law depends has three separate elements: certainty of punishment, celerity (speed) of punishment, and severity of punishment. Late twentieth-century politics focused heavily on severity of punishment, just as England did before Peel eliminated the death penalty for most crime types. This focus had the paradoxical effect of reducing the certainty and celerity of punishment. By admirably increasing the protection of innocent defendants with state-supported counsel and other innovations, the growth of a rule of law focused on avoiding unjust imposition of severe punishment. The barriers that development posed to the certainty of punishment have been debated. Yet few would question the truth of a long delay between arrest and the disposition of a case in most G20 nations' criminal courts.

Deterrence theorists have long suggested that a reversal in emphasis from severity to certainty could produce better results at much lower costs. Powerful evidence for this hypothesis has recently been reported in Hawaii, in the form of Project HOPE (Hawaii's Opportunity and Probation and Enforcement). Begun by Judge Steven Alm of the Honolulu court, the project was aimed at probationers who were ordered to take drug tests. His goal was to cure what he saw as a major problem, one that was crowding the prisons yet failing to prevent crime.

The problem was that too many probationers were being sent to prison for failing their drug tests. Severe penalties could be imposed by judges on any probationer who failed a drug test while on probation; up to five years in prison could be the result. Yet for that reason, probation officers were traditionally reluctant to report any failures of drug tests to the supervising judge. They would often let probationers fail drug tests repeatedly until they eventually reported the fact to the judge. As many as 16 failures were recorded without being reported. Thus on the 17th failure, a probationer might be stunned to find themselves in prison for a long sentence. From a conditioning viewpoint, one may well ask why the 17th offence was worse than the 16th.

The situation in Hawaii was not unique; examples of this pattern may still be found in the revocation of probation or parole in many US states. In Pennsylvania, in the early twenty-first century, some 25 per cent of people entering prisons each year were charged only with a technical violation of parole or probation, not with a new offence. But in that state, like Hawaii, parole and probation officers ignored many violations and made enforcement highly uncertain, but very severe. Judge Alm designed a programme to do just the opposite.

Project HOPE has four key elements. One is that probationers must telephone their probation office every weekday to ask if they were required to come in for a drug test that day. Conventional practice had them scheduled to come in for testing well in advance, but Judge Alm had the exact day of testing randomly selected without notice before the morning probationers were ordered in. The second element was that all drug tests are processed immediately, while the probationer remains in the probation office. The third element is that all drug test failures are punished by immediate jail time, without stopping to appear in court. Only after being marched off to a cell do they appear the next day, or later, before the judge.

The fourth, and most important element, is that the penalties start at a very low level of severity and escalate only gradually. The first drug test failure, for example, earns one night in jail. For offenders who have jobs they might lose if they are jailed immediately, HOPE offers the option of serving the short sentence on the next weekend or next day off from work. A second drug test failure might earn two nights in jail, a third failure three nights, and so on. Moreover, probationers are warned of this penalty structure as soon as they are assigned to HOPE. They are ordered to appear before a judge who delivers the warning that the old pattern will not apply to them: that every failure of a drug test will be punished.

The early results of a randomized field experiment are very encouraging.[19] After two years, offenders assigned to HOPE had half as many arrests for new crimes as those whose drug tests were administered in the pre-HOPE pattern. Over the same time period, the number of days per offender spent in prison was also 50 per cent lower for HOPE probationers than for those on conventional probation. Both crime and costs of justice were cut in half by using less severity, not more. Whether the benefit came from more certainty, however, is not clear. Equally plausible is that the benefit resulted from speed of justice, rather than the probability. For those conventional probationers who failed drug tests even when they were scheduled in advance, there may well have been enough certainty but inadequate celerity. Only by doing more experiments that separate these elements can we answer a vital question in the science of justice.

Offender-Focused Policing

The public image of policing has focused on offenders as police 'targets' both too much and too little. The image has focused too much when it suggests that the main mission for policing is to catch bad guys and prove 'who done it'. The image has focused too little when it ignores the full strategic map of policing to prevent crime. This map includes not only detection of specific offences and prosecution of the offenders responsible for each case. It also includes the strategies of place-focused, victim-focused, and offender-focused policing.[20] All three are prime categories of Problem-Oriented Policing (POP), as articulated by Goldstein[21] as a comprehensive plan by which police can accomplish their mission. The basic POP framework is to focus on patterns of crimes and other problems, organised in any and all ways that are most strategic for reducing the frequency of each pattern or eliminating it altogether.

The most obvious form of offender-focused policing is to identify high-risk offenders coming out of prison, place them under covert surveillance, and catch them in *flagrante delicto*. A randomized field experiment testing this tactic in Washington DC found that it yielded a five-fold increase in the odds of an offender so identified being sent back to prison.[22] Yet this result may be only as useful as the length of time the offender remains in prison. Even then, if the offender could have been pushed towards desistance by less expensive means, re-incarceration may not have been as good news as it appeared in the 1980s.

A broader view of offender-focused policing would address the entire life-course of the offender. Policing is not a stockholder-owned corporation that must focus on short-term profits over long-term value (even if some politicians focus only on the short-term performance of police agencies). To serve the public interest, police may take the long view of how to minimise the harm that each and every individual offender may cause to the public. That is why police in three countries worked with over 3,000 offenders to develop *restorative policing,*[23] by arranging face-to-face conferences between offenders and their victims. The results of twelve experiments in Australia, the US and UK run almost entirely by police agencies (including Scotland Yard and the Australian Federal Police) showed that police can have a substantial impact on repeat offending over a two-year follow-up period.

Restorative policing in these 12 experiments consisted of police assembling and leading meetings of up to three hours. In these meetings, they said little but exercised strong (but soft) power over the discussion. They were all trained to keep the discussion focused on three questions: 1) what happened, 2) who was affected by the crime and how, and 3) what should the offenders do to make up for the harm they have caused the victims? In a room full of friends and relatives of both victims and offenders, a general discussion is held with the police encouraging everyone present to speak. In most cases, offenders express apologies that victims accept as sincere.[24] When an agreement is reached about the steps the offender should take, the meeting adjourns for the officer to write up the terms. That moment is the occasion for a tea or coffee break, in which informal discussion emerges in a general atmosphere of reconciliation.

The results of these experiments show that in ten of the 12 experiments, the frequency of repeat convictions was lower in the cases in which offenders were randomly assigned to restorative justice than in the cases where no conferences occurred. These experiments occurred across a wide range of settings, including:

- diversion from prosecution for both adult and juvenile offenders;

- after conviction but prior to sentencing in adult courts; and

- after sentencing for violent offences to both prison and probation sentences.

The average effect of all these restorative justice conferencing (RJC) experiments shows a statistically significant effect size of 0.1. For experiments involving violent offenders only, the effect size was twice as large, at 0.2. For property crimes, however, there was no statistically discernible difference between cases with and without restorative justice.[25] If these results are generalisable, they suggest that RJC would not be cost-effective for the kind of drug-using property offenders in Project HOPE. Yet there are high volumes of minor to medium-seriousness violent crimes that can be dealt with in this way with good prospects of success. In cases of both property and violent crimes, moreover, restorative policing may prevent crimes of revenge committed by victims against their offenders. A meta-analysis of eight independent tests of restorative justice showed that it reduced the desire for revenge among those victims who police arranged to meet with their offenders.[26] If an officer thinks that victim retaliation might be an issue with any kind of crime, RJC is a potentially effective tool.

These findings suggest that police may well be able to work with offenders in ways other than merely catching them in the act. Envisioning offender-focused policing as a matter of regulation, rather than punishment, may be a useful point of departure.[27] Using the same principles of the 'regulatory pyramid' that are used by Project HOPE, police may be able to impose 'tit-for-tat' rapid but mild responses to any indications of repeat offending. The power of this approach is illustrated by two further experiments in offender-focused policing, which are worthy of naming after a story from before the Common Era.

The Sword of Damocles

The most important evidence suggesting Offender-Desistance Policing comes from two well-designed field experiments in the late 1980s. These experiments found that the mere issuance of a warrant for an offender's arrest had a greater deterrent effect than actually arresting the offender. Both experiments were conducted by the Omaha, Nebraska police responding to calls about minor incidents of domestic violence.

In one experiment, the suspects in the incident were all still present at the scene when police arrived. In the second experiment, the suspects had all left the scene of the alleged crime before the police arrived. When the suspects were present, they were randomly assigned to be arrested or not arrested, but warned in some way.[28] When the suspects were absent, the police either 1) advised the victims how to seek a warrant for the suspect's arrest by going to court the next weekday and paying a fee, or 2) told the victims they would file and pay for a warrant for the arrest of the suspect.[29] In the suspect-still-present experiment, there was no difference in recidivism between the suspects who were arrested and those who were not. But in the suspect-absent experiment, those suspects against whom the police filed warrants had a substantial and statistically significant reduction in recidivism.

These findings, of course, apply only to domestic violence, and perhaps only in Omaha at that period of time. But they also suggest something of potentially widespread application: the hypothesis that a threat to punish is a more powerful deterrent than an actual punishment. This hypothesis is consistent with the classical story of the 'Sword of Damocles'. The story is about a braggart in a royal court who is ordered to dine with the king while sitting under a sharp, heavy sword suspended by a thin silk thread. The king's threat is that if the braggart utters just one boast, the king will order the thread to be cut so that the sword will kill him. The story ends with the braggart eating many, many meals without boasting.

A similar kind of threat may be created by an increase in certainty of police patrols arriving in high-crime 'hot spots'.[30] In a Minneapolis, Minnesota experiment across 110 high-crime locations, 55 locations were chosen to receive police patrols intermittently for an average of 15 per cent of all high-crime hours in those locations. The other 55 received the standard average of seven per cent of those hours in which police patrols were present. The doubling in the certainty of police presence in the experimental places patrolled 15 per cent of the time caused substantially less crime and disorder than in the places patrolled seven per cent of the time.

Combined with the evidence from Hawaii's Project HOPE, these police studies suggest that a threat of taking someone into custody—no matter how minor it may be—can deter offenders against whom the threat is made. Whether they have been hitting a domestic partner, or have been using drugs in violation of probation, or habitually gathering on a street corner where they get into trouble, they may find fairly small increases in added threat to be just enough to stop further offending. The more general form of this proposition is that by communicating more certainty that *some* action will be taken, police can prevent many offences from occurring.

3

Testing the Theory: A Programme of Experiments

Offender-Desistance Policing is an evidence-based crime prevention strategy that requires a programme of experiments to guide it. Unlike most other strategies in the history of policing, ODP depends upon precise knowledge of effective tactics. Using a high standard for what constitutes knowledge, ODP can do best on the basis of randomized controlled trials to choose among a wide and almost infinite range of specific tactics. It can also benefit from continuous improvement in the predictive tools it uses to predict the level of harm each offender may cause the community.

In 1951, the British Attorney General, Lord Shawcross stated that: 'it has never been the rule in this country—I hope that it never will be—that suspected criminal offences must automatically be the subject of prosecution'.[1] That proposition was reaffirmed by the Royal Commission on Criminal Procedure, whose report led to the creation of the Crown Prosecution Service and the current UK arrangements for prosecution.[2] Developing this line,

ODP assumes that the criminal law is only one tool in a police toolbox for solving crime problems.[3] While problem-oriented policing (POP) has rarely considered individual offenders to constitute 'problems' rather than cases, that is only because police have yet to apply the paradigm of life-course criminology to each offender's long-term pattern of offending. Once the many offences committed by the same person are aggregated as a single crime pattern, they clearly constitute a problem within the general meaning of POP. ODP may therefore become a primary application of POP by comprising three key elements:

1. Statistical risk forecasting to determine each offender's harm levels
2. Diversion of low-harm offenders to a 'Damocletian' regulatory regime
3. Maximum prosecution of high-harm offenders

If the evidence and theory underlying this strategy has been correctly interpreted, the central hypothesis it will test is *whether ODP can reduce both the harm from crime and the costs of punishment*. It will do this by making the central focus of policing each offender the achievement of desistance by the most appropriate means in each individual case, including the use of long-term or even life incarceration for the tiny proportion of offenders who are most harmful and least treatable. Rather than viewing each contact with an offender as an isolated case in a closed system of decision making, ODP makes each contact an opportunity to pursue a long-term strategy of pushing or 'nudging' the offender towards desistance from crime.[4]

The broad results of ODP should be greater public safety at less cost than current strategies. By contrast to current British police policies, for example, this will mean much longer prison sentences for a few offenders, while having a much smaller prison population overall—an outcome consistent with the first-year goals of the UK's Coalition Government elected in 2010. By contrast to current US policies, this will mean even greater reductions in prison population and the State-level costs of punishment, which could be translated into State-level funding support for the vast majority of police who are funded by local municipal or county governments. This is a distinct reversal from the current US practice of spending more money on corrections than on police.[5]

In order to develop, test, refine and improve a strategy of ODP, a programme of experiments can best move forward on two parallel tracks. One is to develop the tactics within the strategy, primarily those aimed at low-harm offenders. The other is to develop harm-forecasting tools in each national or regional (local) jurisdiction, based on its distinctive patterns of offending. The latter track is far more time-consuming than the former track, but no less important. Until large numbers of forecasting models[6] can be developed across multiple jurisdictions, it is impossible to say whether a model developed in one jurisdiction can be applied with reasonable accuracy in other jurisdictions. Yet the three tasks required to do so are each complicated and full of obstacles. These tasks consist of:

1. Obtaining tens of thousands of criminal records over at least ten years for each offender

2. Building and testing a forecasting model with non-linear statistical methods

3. Programming the forecasts in police computers where arrestees are processed

Stage 1: First-Offender Experiments

Given the time required for the development of harm forecasts, the Jerry Lee Centre of Experimental Criminology at the University of Cambridge is proceeding first with randomized controlled trials of offender-desistance tactics on arrestees with no prior convictions. By virtually all empirical assessments, first offenders are at low risk of causing high harm. The major exception to this finding is very young offenders (under age 15), especially if they have been arrested for a very serious offence.[7] In the case of suspects over 18 who are arrested for a first offence, there is every reason to treat them as falling into a low-harm category for the purposes of development and testing.

In our first experiment, it is proposed that the police agency will identify all first-offenders who have been arrested for crimes of certain types, generally of low-to-moderate seriousness. Minor assaults, thefts from and of automobiles, and burglary will all be eligible offence categories. An additional requirement is that the supervising officers processing the case for referral to prosecution must decide that the case will be prosecuted, that there is sufficient evidence and it is 'in the public interest' to do so. It is only after this decision has been reached that a diversion to ODP will not constitute 'net-widening'. When cases are randomly assigned to ODP to be compared with cases that are prosecuted, the comparison will focus completely on the kinds of cases that have some potential for the suspect to receive a custodial prison sentence.

At the point that a case is declared ready for prosecution, it will have sufficient evidence needed for a charging decision by a Custody Sergeant. This includes witness or victim statements signed and certified as necessary, physical evidence when available, and DNA analysis or other laboratory reports. At this point, the case will be declared eligible by the supervising officer, who will then enter the identity of the suspect and other details of the eligible case into a secure Cambridge webpage called 'The Cambridge Randomizer,[8] which will instantly compute the random assignment disposition as each case is entered.

If the case is randomly assigned to conventional treatment, the reviewing officer will forward it to the next stage of prosecution review. In this pathway, there is generally a substantial fallout of cases, but still the potential that a defendant may be convicted and sentenced to prison. The exact disposition of each case will vary based on many circumstances. But the average rate of repeat arrest or conviction for new offences can be computed for the entire group from the date that random assignment occurs. If an arrestee, for example, is arrested for committing a new crime while on bail for that offence, it would go into the calculation of recidivism.

If the case is randomly assigned to the 'Damocles Squad', or whatever the police force chooses to call it, there may still be a prosecution. But in this pathway, the arrestee would have an additional choice. The choice would be either to refuse to work with the Damocles Squad and proceed with conventional prosecution, or to agree to work with Damocles on the condition that prosecution will be suspended and eventually dropped if the arrestee complies with all police requirements. Since we predict a high percentage of offenders offered this choice will choose to work with the Damocles Squad, there would be a large difference in the costs and content of official response to the arrest. And, once again, the stopwatch would start running with immediate effect for counting the number of new crimes in the post-random assignment period.

The Damocles procedure would generally proceed as follows:

1. Meet with the arrestee to discuss the instant offence and its implications for his future.

2. Assess the offender's assets for informal social control, including family, education, employment and community organisations.

3. Consider a range of tactical options for the set of conditions that the Damocles Unit will offer the arrestee as a voluntary alternative to prosecution, conditions that may well be in the public interest to prefer over attempts at prosecution.

4. Offer the arrestee the chance to ask questions about the offer, and to consult with a solicitor if the arrestee requests that opportunity.

5. If the arrestee refuses the offer, then the case would be referred for prosecution.

6. If the arrestee accepts the offer, the 'Damocles Unit' would ask the offender to sign the statement of conditions, which would not need to include any admission of guilt for the instant arrest offence. The signature would merely indicate the arrestee's agreement to comply with the conditions, and the police agency's agreement not to prosecute the arrestee for that offence as long as the arrestee complies and does not reoffend. The exact content of the conditions is discussed below in the section on 'specific tactics'.

7. Police would then follow up to ensure compliance with the conditions, basing resources invested on the subjective level of risk the Damocles Unit sees in leaving the arrestee unmonitored. Early monitoring, in any case, could be more intensive, then tapering off as long as the arrestee complies.

Once the samples of about 200 cases are treated with one of the two procedures, the average rates of recidivism in the two groups can be compared. At the same time, the average cost per offender of either prosecuting or diverting the case will be compared, together with other intangible factors such as victim satisfaction. By dividing the cost difference into the recidivism difference, the relative cost-effectiveness of the two approaches can be estimated. The cost of all aspects of the official response after random assignment will be tabulated by the experimenters. The average amount of harm caused by the offenders in the two groups will also be calculated, using sentencing guidelines as the metric (in days of custody) for the weighting of new crimes for which arrestees in each group are arrested in the follow-up period.

Stage 2: Harm-forecasting Experiments

The previous section describes only an experiment in diversion from prosecution for first offenders. Once the harm-forecasting analysis can be provided instantly for each arrestee, a different kind of experiment can be undertaken. The experiment would test not only diversion of low-risk of high-harm arrestees, but also enhanced investigations and prosecutions of high-risk of high-harm arrestees. The comparison would be made by random assignment between cases handled with harm-forecasting risk-assessment or without it.

In these experiments, cases would be eligible based only on instant offence types, and not on offender prior record. Murder and rape cases would likely be excluded, along perhaps with other categories guaranteed to get maximum investigation and prosecution in any event. Less serious offence types would all be included, in order to test the overall impact of harm-forecasting. It is just as important in reducing harm, for example, that a very dangerous person arrested on a very minor offence be given maximum penalties as for a very low-harm person arrested on a fairly serious offence be given a chance to go straight at low cost. Only when incapacitation is likely to last for many years would it be likely to yield a net reduction in harm.[9] Combined with the avoidance of prison for low-harm cases, it would be a very important component of a comparison of the average harm levels across all recidivism in each group.

In these experiments, each arrestee would be screened for eligibility by offence type in the booking and charging area. If the case file for prosecution is completed, the supervising officer would decide (as above) whether the case is eligible. If it is, the case would be referred to the Cambridge Random Assigner.

The detective and prosecution teams would process the cases assigned to conventional treatment. The cases assigned to the Harm-Forecasting Model would immediately be analysed by the model. Those who are deemed high-risk of high-harm would be sent to a case-enhancement unit, a detective team focused on strengthening the evidence in important cases. (What is new about this is the 'Al Capone strategy'—intense investigation of minor offences allegedly committed by high-risk criminals.) The remaining cases would fall into the two other risk-level groups. Those cases not deemed medium-risk of high-harm could be prosecuted in the normal way or referred to the Damocles Unit. Those deemed low-risk of high-harm would be diverted from prosecution immediately or referred to the Damocles Unit. All of the cases, in all three risk levels, would be compared with their average harm of recidivism compared to all of the cases, with no risk assessment, in the control group of conventional treatment.

Stage 3: Specific Tactic Experiments

Once a series of initial experiments has been completed on both the first-offenders and the full range of offender characteristics, a further series of experiments could be undertaken. These experiments would focus on the use of specific police tactics of fostering offender desistance. Some significant evidence to guide this stage should be able to be derived from the experiments in the first two stages—many of the tactics proposed will have formed part of the first offender experiment, even if the primary focus of the evaluation was on the relative effectiveness of charging against ODP. However, this third stage would go beyond a global assessment of the strategies of Damocletian diversion (i.e. conditional suspension of prosecution) and harm-forecasting.

In the experiments on specific tactics, the cases would be screened in two stages. The first stage would be as described above. The second stage would screen for the appropriateness of the specific tactics. For example, if the case involved a violent crime against one or more victims, the case could be appropriate for a restorative justice conference. Yet that tactic would require further screening for both:

1. The arrestee's willingness to meet with victims, and

2. The victims' willingness to meet with arrestees.

Once all the screening is completed for an experiment on the restorative justice conference tactic, the cases would be randomly assigned to have that tactic versus some other standard form of suspended prosecution, such as a nightly curfew, which specifies the time that the arrestees should be inside their residence. Similar experiments could be done with each of the tactics listed below.

Specific Offender-Desistance Tactics: A Summary

Throughout this essay, a series of illustrations has been offered to describe the tactics police can use to help foster desistance from crime. A more comprehensive list can be offered as a summary of the scope of the strategy. Yet no such list should be considered exhaustive. The range of possibilities is infinite, limited only by the development of theory and evidence about effective strategies of offender rehabilitation. Thus the following list is intended to stimulate more proposals, rather than to close the door on any. When viewing criminology as a field of invention,[10] the task at hand is discovery. Our challenge is both to invent and then test untried methods, discarding what does not work and building on what does.

1. **Invoking the Sword of Damocles.** A clear statement of warning to an arrestee about what can happen if they commit another crime is a feature of Project HOPE. It can also be a standard procedure for a Damocles Squad. In Hawaii, every offender assigned to HOPE is called before a judge for a formal warning session. The judge spells out the powers of revocation and potential length of imprisonment, as well as the immed-

iacy with which failures of drug tests will be enforced. Hawken reports that the seven per cent of probationers who failed to appear for these warnings committed most of the new crimes in that arm of the HOPE experiment.[11] Whether that was self-selection, the lack of the warning, or both is impossible to say. But it is a clear precedent in a programme that had overall success, something police can replicate in the initial or final meeting with arrestees when they sign a statement accepting certain conditions.

2. **Door-Knocking.** Police in London, Manchester and elsewhere have a longstanding practice of knocking on the doors of parolees and people on bail. This method of having a conversation with a potentially persisting offender is yet another way to send a deterrent message. At the same time, it can be an opportunity for providing offers of support, or helping ex-offenders deal with other offenders who may be pressing them to continue in crime.

3. **Curfews.** Curfews as part of police bail have been a well-used approach to preventing an offender from being abroad at a time of high risk of or opportunity for offending.

4. **Reporting In.** Much of what probation officers do is to meet with offenders who are required to 'report in' to the probation office. There is no reason why this cannot be an agreement between

police and an arrestee, by which the arrestee comes to meet a Damocles officer once a day, week, month, quarter or year. The mere fact of complying with this condition may be a marker, or reminder, of the arrestee's commitment to comply with all conditions. But it, like door-knocking, may also backfire, interrupting the arrestee's effort to develop a new identity. That is why this tactic, like all tactics, should eventually be tested in isolation from (or in comparison to) other offender-desistance tactics.

5. **Voluntary Drug or Alcohol Treatment.** Many court-based programmes try to get some offenders to attend and complete drug or alcohol treatment programmes. The powers of the court to enforce compliance with certainty and speed may not always be adequate to the task. Police may be in a much better position to encourage drug users to comply with their treatment regime and attend all their mandated sessions.

6. **Voluntary Trauma Treatment.** Many offenders suffer from post-traumatic stress, which may in turn drive their addiction to drugs or other intoxicants, motivating them to commit crimes to buy intoxicants. Arranging for treatment by Prolonged Exposure Therapy (PET), a form of cognitive behavioural therapy, may be a way to deal with an underlying cause of crime. One offender in Cambridge, for example, had not

been a drug addict until he was gang-raped in a young offenders' institution at age 16. His drug use (cocaine) since then had been his primary motivation for a crime pattern of serial burglaries. When this was discovered, Cambridgeshire Police attempted to arrange post-trauma therapy for him.

7. **Restorative Justice.** There is evidence that police themselves can lead these conferences with high satisfaction levels among both victims and offenders. The evidence also clearly shows that such conferences help offenders to desist from crime, in cost-effective terms relative to the cost of the conferences.[12]

8. **Offender Relocation.** Kirk examined the reoffending rates of offenders displaced by Hurricane Katrina.[13] He reports that less than half as many ex-prisoners went back to prison in one year if they moved to a different community than if they went back to New Orleans. In England today, some police and private charities are arranging relocation for some offenders, with reports of sharply reduced frequency of repeat offending. While this tactic may be too resource-intensive to employ for less frequent offenders, it could be the method of choice for low-harm property offenders who are prolific and persistent.

4

Summary and Conclusions

It is entirely possible that all of these tactics could fail to foster desistance from crime, even though the strategy of diversion or harm-forecasting could work nonetheless. There may be more general validity in the finding by Petrosino and his colleagues[1] that doing nothing with juveniles was better than doing something, at least in terms of repeat offending. Yet it is very difficult to reconcile doing nothing with deeply held moral values for holding offenders accountable. Whatever works in terms of helping offenders desist should also be seen as a form of justice, one by which offenders must pay a price.

Whether it is acceptable for police, and not courts, to decide what is justice, has been a grey area for centuries. The decision not to prosecute in the public interest is a longstanding power of the constable. A decision to work out an informal restitution between offender and victim, outside the King's justice, has thousands of years of precedent. The modern view that police investigate and courts decide is manifestly untrue according to current statistics in England and Wales: almost equal numbers of criminal cases are dealt with out of court (by police) and in court. Whether those decisions are right, and whether they should be based on harm-forecasting, are matters that can be addressed by the broader research programme at the Cambridge Institute of Criminology.

The programme of experiments described in this chapter is more focused. It merely asks whether the invention of certain and swift regulation of compliance with the law is possible when implemented by the police. It relies on major police agencies to address the legal and policy issues, in a country that may soon have elected Police and Crime Commissioners. It also relies on criminological theory and evidence to design the tactics that have the most promise for Offender-Desistance Policing. If it succeeds in even completing the experiments, the programme will be worthwhile.

References

Ariel, Barak, Jordi, Vila and Sherman, Lawrence, 'Random Assignment Without Tears: How I learned to Stop Worrying and Love the Cambridge Randomizer', Unpublished manuscript, Jerry Lee Centre for Experimental Criminology, Institute of Criminology, Cambridge University, 2011.

Barnes, Geoffrey C., Ahlman, Lindsay, Gill, Charlotte, Sherman, Lawrence W., Kurtz, Ellen and Malvestuto, Robert, 'Low-intensity community supervision for low-risk offenders: a randomized, controlled trial', *Journal of Experimental Criminology* 6: 159–189, 2010.

Barrie, David, *Police in the Age of Improvement: police development and the civic tradition in Scotland, 1775-1865*, Cullompton, Devon: Willan Publishing, 2008.

Berk, Richard, Sherman, Lawrence, Barnes, Geoffrey, Ahlman, Lindsay, Kurtz, Ellen and Malvestuto, Robert, 'Forecasting Murder within a Population of Probationers and Parolees: a high stakes application of statistical learning', *Journal of the Royal Statistical Society: Series A (Statistics in Society)* 172: 191–211, 2009.

Braithwaite, John, *Restorative Justice and Responsive Regulation*, New York: Oxford University Press, 2002.

Colquhoun, Patrick (1806), *A Treatise on the Police of the Metropolis*, 7th edition, reprinted 1969 at Montclair, New Jersey: Patterson-Smith Publishers.

Cullen, Francis T., 'Rehabilition and Treatment Programs', in Wilson, James Q. and Petersilia, Joan (eds), *Crime: public policies for crime control,* Oakland, Cal: ICS Press, 2002, pp. 253-611.

Dubber, Markus Dirk, 'Theories of Crime and Punishment in German Criminal Law', Buffalo Legal Studies Research Paper Series, Paper No. 2005-02, 2005; Social Science Research Network Electronic Paper Collection at http://ssrn.com/abstract=829226.

Dunford, Franklyn, 'System-initiated Warrants for Suspects of Misdemeanor Domestic Assault: A pilot study', *Justice Quarterly* 7: 631-653, 1990.

Dunford, Franklyn, Huizinga, David and Elliot, Delbert, 'The Role of Arrest in Domestic Assault: The Omaha Police Experiment', *Criminology* 28: 183-206, 1990.

Durlauf, Steven N. and Nagin, Daniel, 'Imprisonment and Crime: Can Both be Reduced?', *Criminology and Public Policy* 10: 13-54, 2011.

Goldstein, Herman, 'Improving Policing: A Problem-Oriented Approach', *Crime and Delinquency*, 25: 236-258, 1979.

Goldstein, Herman, *Problem-Oriented Policing*, New York: McGraw-Hill, 1990.

Hawken, Angela, 'Reducing Imprisonment With Certainty on Probation Violations: Project HOPE', Paper Presented to the 11th Jerry Lee Symposium on Crime

Prevention, United States Senate Russell Office Building, 2 May 2011.

Kirk, David S., 'A Natural Experiment on Residential Change and Recidivism: Lessons from Hurricane Katrina', *American Sociological Review* 74: 484-505, 2009.

Kirk, David, 'Residential Change as a Turning Point in the Life Course of Crime: Desistance or Temporary Cessation?', Austin, Texas: Unpublished MS., Dept of Sociology, University of Texas, 2011.

Kleiman, Mark, *When Brute Force Fails: How to Have Less Crime and Less Punishment*, Princeton: Princeton University Press, 2009.

Laub, John, Remarks to the 11th Jerry Lee Symposium on Crime Prevention, United States Senate Russell Office Building, 2 May 2011.

Laub, John and Sampson, Robert, 'Understanding Desistance from Crime', in *Crime and Justice: A Review of Research*, Chicago: University of Chicago Press, 2001, pp. 1-69.

Laub, John and Sampson, Robert, *Shared Beginnings, Divergent Lives: delinquent boys to age 70*, Cambridge, Mass: Harvard University Press, 2003.

Lentz, Susan and Chaires, Robert H., 'The Invention of Peel's Principles: a study of policing "textbook" history', *Journal of Criminal Justice*, Volume 35: 69-79, 2007.

REFERENCES

Losel, Friedrich, 'Treatment and Management of Psychopaths', in Cooke, David J., Forth, Adelle E. and Hare, Robert (eds), *Psychopathy: theory, research, and implications for society*, Dordrecht, The Netherlands: Kluwer, 1998, pp. 303-54.

Martin, Susan E. and Sherman, Lawrence W., 'Selective Apprehension: A Police Strategy For Repeat Offenders', *Criminology* Vol. 24, No. 1, February 1986, pp. 155-173.

Meehl, Paul E., *Clinical versus Statistical Prediction: a theoretical analysis and a review of the evidence*, Minneapolis, MN: University of Minnesota Press, 1954.
Nagin, Daniel S., Cullen, Francis T. and Jonson, Cheryl Leo, 'Imprisonment and Reoffending', in Michael Tonry, Michael (ed.), *Crime and Justice*, Chicago: University of Chicago Press, 2009.

National Research Council, Panel on Research on Policing, Skogan, Wesley and Frdyl, K. (eds), *Fairness and Effectiveness in Policing: the evidence*, Washington, DC: National Academies Press, 2004.

Nieuwbeerta, Paul, Nagin, Daniel and Blokland, Arjan A.J., 'Assessing the Impact of First-Time Imprisonment on Offenders' Subsequent Criminal Career Development: a matched samples comparison', *Journal of Quantitative Criminology*, 2009.

Petrosino, Anthony, Turpin-Petrosino, Carolyn and Guckenburg, Sarah, *Formal System Processing of Juveniles: effects on delinquency*, Campbell Collaboration, 2010; campbellcollaboration.org/lib/download/761/

Phillips, C., *Royal Commission on Criminal Procedure,* London: HMSO, Cmnd 8092, 1981.

Sampson, Robert and Laub, John, *Crime in the Making: Pathways and Turning Points Through Life,* Cambridge, Mass: Harvard University Press, 1993.

Shapland, Joanna, Atkinson, Anne, Atkinson, Helen, Dignan, James, Edwards, Lucy, Hibbert, Jeremy, Howes, Marie, Johnstone, Jennifer, Robinson, Gwen and Sorsby, Angela, 'Does Restorative Justice Affect Reconviction? The fourth report from the evaluation of three schemes', London: Ministry of Justice, 2008.

Sherman, Lawrence W., 'Attacking Crime: Police and Crime Control', in Morris, Norval and Tonry, Michael (eds), *Modern Policing: crime and justice*, Chicago: University of Chicago Press, Vol. 15, 1992, pp. 159-230.

Sherman, Lawrence, 'Reason for Emotion: Reinventing Justice with Theories, Innovations and Research. 2002 ASC Presidential Address', *Criminology* 41 (1): 1-38, 2003.

Sherman, Lawrence W., Strang, Heather, Angel, Caroline, Woods, Daniel, Rossner, Meredith, Barnes, Geoffrey C., Bennett, Sarah and Inkpen, Nova, 'Effects of Face-to-Face Restorative Justice on Victims of Crime in Four Randomized, Controlled Trials', *Journal of Experimental Criminology* (1:3) 367-395, 2005.

Sherman, Lawrence W., 'To Develop and Test: the inventive difference between evaluation and experimentation', *Journal of Experimental Criminology* 2(3): 393-406, 2006.

Sherman, Lawrence W., 'Preventing Murder With Special Units in Probation and Parole Agencies', *Criminology and Public Policy* 6: 843-849, 2007.

Sherman, Lawrence W., 'The Power Few Hypothesis: experimental criminology and the reduction of harm', *Journal of Experimental Criminology* 3: 299-321, 2007.

Sherman, Lawrence W., 'Less Prison, More Police, Less Crime: how criminology can save the States from bankruptcy', Washington, DC: National Institute of Justice Video posted at:
http://nij.ncjrs.gov/multimedia/video-sherman.htm

Sherman, Lawrence W., 'Al Capone, the Sword of Damocles, and the Police–Corrections Budget Ratio', *Criminology & Public Policy*, 10: 195-206, 2011.

Sherman, Lawrence W., 'Criminology as Invention', in Bosworth, M. and Hoyle, C. (eds), *What is Criminology?*, Oxford: Oxford University Press, 2011, pp. 423-39.

Sherman, Lawrence W. and Weisburd, David, 'General Deterrent Effects of Police Patrol in Crime Hot Spots: a randomized, controlled trial', *Justice Quarterly*, Vol. 12, No. 4: 635-648, 1995.

Sherman, Lawrence W. and Strang, Heather, *Restorative Justice: the Evidence*, London: The Smith Institute. 2007.

Sherman, Lawrence W. and Strang, Heather, 'Restorative Justice as a Psychological Treatment: healing victims, reintegrating offenders', in Towl, Graham and Crighton, David (eds), *Handbook of Forensic Psychology*, London: BPS Blackwell, 2010, pp. 398-415.

Strang, Heather, Lawrence Sherman and Woods, Daniel J., 'Effects of Restorative Justice Conferences on Victims and Offenders: a systematic review', Paper presented to the Campbell Collaboration Annual Conference, Oslo, Norway, May 2009.

Thaler, Richard and Sunstein, Cass, *Nudge: improving decisions about health, wealth, and happiness*, New Haven, Conn: Yale University Press, 2008.

Von Liszt, Franz, Der Zweckgedanke im Strafrecht, in 3 ZStW 1, 1883.

Commentary

Ken Pease

I was very pleased that Civitas asked me to write a commentary on the Sherman/Neyroud paper on Offender-Desistance Policing because I am a fervent admirer of both authors. Larry Sherman has brought an enviable energy and evidence focus to British policing. The immense value of Peter Neyroud's tenure heading the National Policing Improvement Agency has yet to be acknowledged. In time, it will be.

Having read the piece, I avoided writing this commentary for two weeks, finding compelling reasons to take the dogs for extra walks, rearrange the spice jars, anything to avoid the painful act of putting on record my points of disagreement with people I greatly admire. One must, however, call it as one sees it.

As to the design of the proposed field studies, this is impeccable, as is to be expected given their *onlie begetters*. I have, nevertheless, three substantial concerns.

1. The concept of desistance-based policing involves a wholesale shift of responsibility from prosecutors and courts to the police. As the paper's authors note 'Whether it is acceptable for police, and not courts, to decide what is justice, has been a grey area for centuries'. In practice, criminal justice policy, covert and overt, has for many years involved a massive and increasing filtering of the criminally active population so that courts and prisons are presented with a volume of cases which leaves them *just* able to cope.

The police already exercise a form of triage on the streets, with some offences being ignored, others dealt with informally, and a minority leading to further action, which may include formal caution.[1] Experienced officers develop a perceptual shorthand concerning what constitutes the 'normal' and 'deviant' levels of criminality in their areas, ultimately deploying their legal powers only in instances they perceive as exceeding the 'normal deviance' threshold. Because of the high demand on the police service, officers in crime-ridden areas have a higher threshold of 'normal' deviance and thus intervene in substantially fewer acts of lower-level deviance than their peers working in low-crime locales. Any use or extension of police discretionary decision making is likely to increase the already grotesque inter-area variation in crimes suffered. Police services have grown internal bureaucracies staffed by investigation managers (including sergeants and civilian staff) so as to weed out cases before referring the remainder onwards to the Crown Prosecution Service, which in turn applies rigorous charging standards, not proceeding with many cases. Eventually, alleged offenders who have survived all the forgoing case culls go to court. This repeatedly filtered group, once found or pleading guilty, face courts with an armoury of sanctions including those, like suspended sentences, which involve no further active intervention in the lives of those sentenced, and whose breach cannot be guaranteed to trigger any more rigorous action.

Imposing on the police service the responsibilities implied by desistance policing (together with the allocation of blame when things go wrong) places substantial direct and opportunity costs on police forces. I shared the paper with a front-line police officer without indicating my view. He replied in writing: 'The paper seems to be placing all matters of sorting out crime in all forms... squarely at the feet of the police. I would say that a lot of the suggestions are either already being done in one form or another by a particular agency or are not in the remit of the police.'

2. Crime may be addressed by, on the one hand, changing the inclinations (or availability to offend) of those disposed to commit it, or alternatively by manipulating the environment so as to change the threshold at which the urge to act is translated into action. The second approach is generally known as situational crime prevention (SCP). Many published examples exist of successful initiatives of this kind, and SCP is what prudent businesses and individuals

already do to protect themselves from crime. The primary advantage of SCP is that it concerns itself with all crime experienced by victims, not the small minority which results in a meaningful sanction.[2]

With finite resources, and the almost universal political inclination to equate the problem of crime with the treatment of criminals, SCP tends to be neglected. For example, home security, demonstrably effective in reducing victimisation, is currently being marginalised in the Government's rush to build affordable homes. The street layout of new developments is important in determining levels of crime suffered.[3] A linked strand of research on the spatio-temporal distribution of crime[4] offers scope for the prediction of crime locations and in consequence preventive patrolling and the prevention of repeat victimisation.

3. The issue of repeat victimisation is of crucial importance. An emphasis on the prevention of very serious crimes such as murder marginalises the importance of repeated low-level crime to the misery of individuals in crime-challenged communities. The Leicestershire case of Fiona Pilkington, who killed herself and her daughter rather than face continued low-level offending is unique only in the recognition of the effects of chronic low-level crime and disorder that it evoked. The sequence of repeated calls to the police, tragic outcome and Chief Constable's admission that 'we let the family down' has become drearily familiar.

In short, while the Sherman and Neyroud approach is feasible and will be elegantly designed and conducted with scrupulous care and analytic brilliance, in my view it improperly relocates responsibility for the disposition of offenders onto the police service, imposes an opportunity cost in terms of police time which could be better deployed in preventive design and patrolling of places, and neglects the cumulative misery of repeated low-level victimisation.

References

Farrington, D.P. and Jolliffe, D., 'Crime and Justice in England and Wales, 1981-1999', in Tonry M. and Farrington, D.P. *Crime and Punishment in Western Countries 1980-1999*, Chicago: University of Chicago Press, 2005.

Johnson, S. and Bowers, K., 'Permeability and Crime Risk: Are cul-de-sacs safer?' *Journal of Quantitative Criminology* 26(1) 89-111, 2010.

Klinger, David A., 'Negotiating Order in Patrol Work: An Ecological Theory of Police Response to Deviance', *Criminology* 35 (2):277-306, 1997.

Mohler, G. *et al.*, 'Self-Exciting Point Process Modeling of Crime', *Journal of the American Statistical Association*, 106 (493) 100-108, 2011.

Notes

1: Policing and Criminal Justice Context in 2011

1   Criminal Justice Joint Inspectorates, *Exercising Discretion: the gateway to justice*, HMIC, 2011; electronic paper at http://www.hmic.gov.uk/SiteCollectionDocuments/Joint%20Inspections/CJI_20110609.pdf

2   Sherman, Lawrence W. and Strang, Heather, *Restorative Justice: the Evidence*, London: The Smith Institute, 2007.

2: Offender-Desistance Policing

1   Laub, John and Sampson, Robert, *Shared Beginnings, Divergent Lives: delinquent boys to age 70*, Cambridge, Mass: Harvard University Press, 2003.

2   Laub, John and Sampson, Robert, 'Understanding Desistance from Crime', in *Crime and Justice: a review of research*, Chicago: University of Chicago Press, 2001, pp. 1-69.

3   National Research Council, Panel on Research on Policing, Skogan, Wesley and Frdyl, K. (eds), *Fairness and Effectiveness in Policing: the evidence*, Washington, DC: National Academies Press, 2004.

4   Sherman, Lawrence W., 'The Power Few Hypothesis: experimental criminology and the reduction of harm', *Journal of Experimental Criminology* 3: 299-321, 2007.

5   Berk, Richard, Sherman, Lawrence, Barnes, Geoffrey, Ahlman, Lindsay, Kurtz, Ellen and Malvestuto, Robert, 'Forecasting Murder within a Population of

Probationers and Parolees: a high stakes application of statistical learning', *Journal of the Royal Statistical Society: Series A (Statistics in Society)* 172: 191–211, 2009.

6 Barnes, Geoffrey, 'Applying the Berk Model to a Population of Philadelphia Offenders', Philadelphia: Unpublished Powerpoint Presentation, Jerry Lee Center of Criminology, University of Pennsylvania, 2007.

7 Berk *et al.*, 'Forecasting Murder within a Population of Probationers and Parolees', 2009.

8 Meehl, Paul E., *Clinical versus Statistical Prediction: a theoretical analysis and a review of the evidence*, Minneapolis, MN: University of Minnesota Press, 1954.

9 Sherman, Lawrence W., 'The Power Few Hypothesis: experimental criminology and the reduction of harm', *Journal of Experimental Criminology* 3: 299-321, 2007.

10 Sherman, Lawrence W., 'Preventing Murder With Special Units in Probation and Parole Agencies', *Criminology and Public Policy* 6: 843-849, 2007.

11 Barnes, Geoffrey C., Ahlman, Lindsay, Gill, Charlotte, Sherman, Lawrence W., Kurtz, Ellen and Malvestuto, Robert, 'Low-intensity Community Supervision for Low-risk offenders: a randomized, controlled trial', *Journal of Experimental Criminology* 6: 159–189, 2010.

12 Petrosino, Anthony, Turpin-Petrosino, Carolyn and Guckenburg, Sarah, *Formal System Processing of Juveniles: effects on delinquency*, Campbell

Collaboration, 2010;
campbellcollaboration.org/lib/download/761/

13 Laub and Sampson, 'Understanding Desistance from Crime', 2001; Laub and Sampson, *Shared Beginnings, Divergent Lives*, 2003.

14 Petrosino, *et al.*, *Formal System Processing of Juveniles: effects on delinquency*, 2010.

15 Nagin, Daniel S., Cullen, Francis T. and Jonson, Cheryl Leo, 'Imprisonment and Reoffending', in Michael Tonry, Michael (ed.), *Crime and Justice*, Chicago: University of Chicago Press, 2009; Nieuwbeerta, Paul, Nagin, Daniel and Blokland, Arjan A. J., 'Assessing the Impact of First-Time Imprisonment on Offenders' Subsequent Criminal Career Development: a matched samples comparison', *Journal of Quantitative Criminology*, 2009; Durlauf, Steven N. and Nagin, Daniel, 'Imprisonment and Crime: can both be reduced?', *Criminology and Public Policy* 10: 13-54, 2011.

16 Laub and Sampson, *Shared Beginnings, Divergent Lives*, 2003.

17 Laub and Sampson, *Shared Beginnings, Divergent Lives*, 2003.

18 Nieuwbeerta, Paul, Nagin, Daniel and Blokland, Arjan A. J., 'Assessing the Impact of First-Time Imprisonment on Offenders' Subsequent Criminal Career Development: a matched samples comparison', *Journal of Quantitative Criminology*, 2009.

19 Hawken, Angela, 'Reducing Imprisonment With Certainty on Probation Violations: Project HOPE', Paper Presented to the 11th Jerry Lee Symposium on Crime Prevention, United States Senate Russell Office Building, 2 May 2011.

20 Sherman, Lawrence W., 'Attacking Crime: police and crime control', in Norval Morris, Norval and Tonry, Michael (eds), *Modern Policing: crime and justice*, Chicago: University of Chicago Press, Vol. 15, 1992, pp. 159-230.

21 Goldstein, Herman, 'Improving Policing: A Problem-Oriented Approach', *Crime and Delinquency*, 25: 236-258, 1979; Goldstein, Herman, *Problem-Oriented Policing*, New York: McGraw-Hill, 1990.

22 Martin, Susan E. and Sherman, Lawrence W., 'Selective Apprehension: A Police Strategy For Repeat Offenders', *Criminology* Vol. 24, No. 1, February 1986, pp. 155-73.

23 Sherman, Lawrence W. and Strang, Heather, *Restorative Justice: the Evidence,* London: The Smith Institute, 2007.

24 Sherman, Lawrence W., Strang, Heather, Angel, Caroline, Woods, Daniel, Rossner, Meredith, Barnes, Geoffrey C., Bennett, Sarah and Inkpen, Nova, 'Effects of Face-to-Face Restorative Justice on Victims of Crime in Four Randomized, Controlled Trials', *Journal of Experimental Criminology* (1:3) 367-395, 2005.

25 Strang, Heather, Sherman, Lawrence and Woods, Daniel J., 'Effects of Restorative Justice Conferences on

Victims and Offenders: A Systematic Review', Paper presented to the Campbell Collaboration Annual Conference, Oslo, Norway, May, 2009.

26 Sherman, *et al.*, 'Effects of Face-to-Face Restorative Justice on Victims of Crime in Four Randomized, Controlled Trials', 2005.

27 Braithwaite, John, *Restorative Justice and Responsive Regulation*, New York: Oxford University Press, 2002.

28 Dunford, Franklyn, Huizinga, David and Elliot, Delbert, 'The Role of Arrest in Domestic Assault: The Omaha Police Experiment', *Criminology* 28: 183-206, 1990.

29 Dunford *et al.*, 'The Role of Arrest in Domestic Assault: The Omaha Police Experiment', 1990.

30 Sherman, Lawrence W. and Weisburd, David, 'General Deterrent Effects of Police Patrol in Crime Hot Spots: a randomized, controlled trial', *Justice Quarterly*, Vol. 12, No. 4: 635-648, 1995.

3: Testing the Theory: A Programme of Experiments

1   Criminal Justice Joint Inspectorates, *Exercising Discretion: the gateway to justice*, HMIC, 2011:3; electronic paper at http://www.hmic.gov.uk/SiteCollectionDocuments/Joint%20Inspections/CJI_20110609.pdf

2   Phillips, C., *Royal Commission on Criminal Procedure*, London: HMSO, Cmnd 8092, 1981.

3 Goldstein, Herman, 'Improving Policing: a problem-oriented approach', *Crime and Delinquency*, 25: 236-258, 1979; Goldstein, Herman, *Problem-Oriented Policing*, New York: McGraw-Hill, 1990.

4 Thaler, Richard and Sunstein, Cass, *Nudge: improving decisions about health, wealth, and happiness*, New Haven, Conn: Yale University Press, 2008.

5 Sherman, Lawrence W., 'Al Capone, the Sword of Damocles, and the Police–Corrections Budget Ratio', *Criminology & Public Policy*, 10: 195-206, 2011.

6 E.g. Berk, Richard, Sherman, Lawrence, Barnes, Geoffrey, Ahlman, Lindsay, Kurtz, Ellen and Malvestuto, Robert, 'Forecasting Murder within a Population of Probationers and Parolees: a high stakes application of statistical learning', *Journal of the Royal Statistical Society: Series A (Statistics in Society)* 172: 191-211, 2009.

7 Berk, *et al.*, 'Forecasting Murder within a Population of Probationers and Parolees', 2009.

8 Ariel, Barak, Jordi, Vila and Sherman, Lawrence, 'Random Assignment Without Tears: How I learned to Stop Worrying and Love the Cambridge Randomizer', Unpublished manuscript, Jerry Lee Centre for Experimental Criminology, Institute of Criminology, Cambridge University, 2011.

9 Nagin, Daniel S., Cullen, Francis T. and Jonson, Cheryl Leo, 'Imprisonment and Reoffending', in Tonry, Michael (ed.), *Crime and Justice*, Chicago: University of Chicago Press, 2009.

10 Sherman, Lawrence W., 'Criminology as Invention', in Bosworth, M. and Hoyle, C. (eds), *What is Criminology?*, Oxford: Oxford University Press, 2011, pp. 423-39.

11 Hawken, Angela, 'Reducing Imprisonment With Certainty on Probation Violations: Project HOPE', Paper Presented to the 11th Jerry Lee Symposium on Crime Prevention, United States Senate Russell Office Building, 2 May 2011.

12 Shapland, Joanna, Atkinson, Anne, Atkinson, Helen, Dignan, James, Edwards, Lucy, Hibbert, Jeremy, Howes, Marie, Johnstone, Jennifer, Robinson, Gwen and Sorsby, Angela, 'Does Restorative Justice Affect Reconviction? The fourth report from the evaluation of three schemes', London: Ministry of Justice, 2008.

13 Kirk, David S., 'A Natural Experiment on Residential Change and Recidivism: lessons from Hurricane Katrina', *American Sociological Review* 74: 484-505, 2009.

4: Summary and Conclusions

1 Petrosino, Anthony, Turpin-Petrosino, Carolyn and Guckenburg, Sarah, *Formal System Processing of Juveniles: effects on delinquency*, Campbell Collaboration, 2010; campbellcollaboration.org/lib/download/761/

Commentary

1 Klinger, David A., 'Negotiating Order in Patrol Work: an ecological theory of police response to deviance', *Criminology* 35 (2):277-306, 1997.

2   See for example Farrington, D.P. and Jolliffe, D.,
    'Crime and Justice in England and Wales, 1981-1999',
    in Tonry M. and Farrington, D.P. *Crime and Punishment
    in Western Countries 1980-1999*, Chicago: University of
    Chicago Press, 2005.

3   See for example, Johnson, S. and Bowers, K.,
    'Permeability and Crime Risk: are cul-de-sacs safer?'
    Journal of Quantitative Criminology 26(1) 89-111, 2010.

4   See e.g., Mohler, G. *et al.*, 'Self-Exciting Point Process
    Modeling of Crime', *Journal of the American Statistical
    Association*, 106 (493) 100-108, 2011.